GHOSTLY TALES FROM LONG AGO

Peter Hepplewhite &
Neil Tonge

MACDONALD YOUNG BOOKS

CONTENTS

• • • • • ◻ Introduction   5

• • • • • ◻ Joan of Arc – Saint or Sinner?   6

• • • • • ◻ The Haunted House of Ancient Athens   11

• • • • • ◻ The Tragedy of Catherine Howard   16

• • • • • ◻ The Phantom Soldiers of Edgehill   21

• • • • • ◻ Comfort's Curse   26

• • • • • ◻ Glossary   30

• • • • • ◻ Index   31

Do you believe in ghosts, spirits or people with special psychic powers? This book looks at how curious happenings connected with key historical events and personalities may have changed the course of history – forever.

Stories of the supernatural raise lots of questions. The five stories you are about to read are no exception – they ask some spine-chilling questions about the past:

When Joan of Arc claimed to have been given a divine message that could save her country, was she speaking the truth, or was she guilty of conspiring with the devil?

Should the Greek philosopher Athendorus have rented a haunted house, and what should he have done about the ghost's dreadful message?

Can the ghost of Queen Catherine Howard really be seen running down the Long Gallery at Hampton Court Palace, begging for mercy from her cruel husband, King Henry VIII? Or does the vision take place in the minds of visitors touched by her tragic story?

At Edgehill, terrified witnesses claim to have seen phantom soldiers fighting the first grim battle of the English Civil War in 1642. Can terrible events imprint themselves on their surroundings and replay just like a video tape?

Comfort Ainsley was hanged as a witch in 1692 – but was she really an evil woman guilty of witchcraft, or a victim of prejudice and fear?

Before you make up your mind about these stories, weigh up the evidence in the History Fact Files and check out the original photographs that provide the facts behind the fiction.

Only when you have studied all the evidence and decided for yourself will this history rest in peace!

JOAN OF ARC – SAINT OR SINNER?

A FRIEND OF THE DEVIL?

It is May 1431. Inside the gloomy great hall of the castle at Rouen, in France, a trial is taking place. Around the walls, whispering together on rows of benches, are priests and monks. On a raised platform at one end of the hall sits Pierre Cauchon, Bishop of Beauvais. But who is the prisoner? Who could be so dangerous as to require such a powerful court as this? And why is the castle protected by heavily armed English soldiers?

A nineteen-year-old girl sits awkwardly on a stool in front of the bishop. She is chained to a large block of wood and there is an English soldier guarding her. The soldier pulls her roughly to her feet and she faces the court. This is Joan of Arc, who is accused of conspiring with the devil to bring about the deaths of many men. Is she innocent or guilty?

SAVING THE KINGDOM

The Battle of Agincourt. Victories such as this secured England's hold on large areas of France.

Early in the fifteenth century, France was a troubled country. For over three hundred years the English kings had ruled lands not only in England but in France too. English kings had married French princesses and gained even more land. At times the English kings controlled more French land than the King of France himself. Different regions of France were ruled by powerful landowners. The Duke of Burgundy, who often sided with the English kings, was the most powerful landowner in France at the time.

Wars between France and England had begun in 1337 and dragged on for more than a hundred years. At Agincourt in 1415, many powerful French nobles were killed in battle against Henry V of England, who won a great victory.

The French kingdom began to collapse. The French king, Charles VI, was judged to be insane. His wife, Queen Isabelle, offered their daughter, Catherine, in marriage to the triumphant Henry V. Nobody considered Charles VI's son, a young man aged twenty and also named Charles. He was weak and had few supporters. All he had left of his kingdom was some territory south of the River Loire.

In 1422 Henry V died from a disease that he had caught while trying to win yet more land in France. His son was only a baby and there now seemed to be a chance for France to fight back. But Charles VII made only half-hearted efforts to regain his lands. It was at this moment that help came from an unlikely source – a young peasant girl.

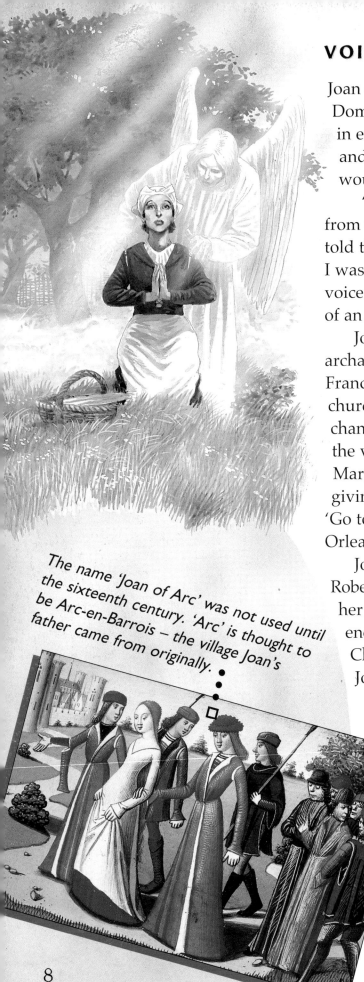

VOICES FROM GOD?

Joan of Arc was born into a farming family in Domremy, a village on the borders of Lorraine in eastern France. She was a religious child and while other children were playing, she would kneel in the fields praying to God.

'I was thirteen when I first heard a voice from God giving me help and guidance,' Joan told the court. 'It was midday, in the summer. I was in my father's garden. When I heard the voice again I recognized that it was the voice of an angel.'

Joan believed that the voice belonged to the archangel St Michael, the warrior saint of France. He told her to be good and to go to church regularly. Then the messages began to change. The archangel's voice was joined by the voices of two other saints, Catherine and Margaret. These voices came more often, giving her a message she could not ignore: 'Go to France, Joan. Rescue the people of Orleans from the besieging English.'

Joan went to see the local nobleman, Sir Robert de Baudricourt. She asked him to provide her with an escort to take her safely through enemy territory so that she could meet King Charles VII at his castle in Chinon. When Joan arrived there, she knelt before the king. 'Most noble lord, I have been sent by God to bring help to you and your kingdom and I will prove this by rescuing the besieged people of Orleans,' she declared. Amazingly, Joan managed to convince the king and the bishops that her mission was genuine. A banner and a special suit of armour were prepared for her. Leading an army of 12,000 men, Joan marched on Orleans at the end of April 1429.

The name 'Joan of Arc' was not used until the sixteenth century. 'Arc' is thought to be Arc-en-Barrois – the village Joan's father came from originally.

In her shining armour and with her unshakeable belief in God's calling, Joan inspired the troops to fight. Within ten days the French army had driven the English from Orleans. For the next twelve months, town after town surrendered to Joan's army.

THE TRIAL

The English soldiers had become increasingly frightened of Joan. They believed that she had supernatural powers, which were enabling her to win victory after victory. But in 1430 as she was leading an attack on the English, Joan was captured and handed over to the Duke of Burgundy's troops. The Burgundians sold Joan to their English allies.

Joan was put on trial by the English. She defended herself with great courage but was found guilty of heresy. On 30 May 1431 in the market-place at Rouen, Joan was tied to a stake and burned alive. One person who witnessed her death recalled, 'I heard a priest say, when he was returning from the execution, groaning and weeping sadly, "We have burned a saint."'

A VISION IN THE MARKET-PLACE

In 1918 Alan Ainscough, an English soldier fighting in France during the First World War, had a strange experience in Rouen. As he walked through the town he felt himself marching at the head of a column of soldiers dressed in armour. In their midst was a young girl. At the end of the street was the market-place, and Alan read on a plaque above the pavement that this was the place where Joan of Arc had died – a fact that he had not known until that day.

Many pictures of Joan painted since her death show her as a martyr.

HISTORY **FACT FILE**

✝ **In 1456**, twenty-five years after Joan's execution, another trial at Rouen concluded that Joan of Arc had been a good Christian, not a heretic. In 1920 Joan was recognized as a saint by the Catholic Church.

✝ **St Joan** became a special protector of France. When the country was occupied by the Germans during the Second World War, the French people who fought on against Germany used the Cross of Lorraine (the region where Joan was born) as their symbol of resistance. They shared Joan's aim – to rid France of foreign rule.

THE HAUNTED HOUSE OF ANCIENT ATHENS

THE GREATNESS OF ATHENS

Ancient Greece was never a united country. The Greeks belonged to different city-states. Each city-state had its own army, main town and government. The city-states fought each other often but during the fifth century BC one of them, Athens, became the most powerful.

Athens was famous for its art and architecture, and its philosophers. These great thinkers laid the foundations of many modern sciences such as medicine, mathematics and biology. In Ancient Greek the word 'philosopher' means 'lover of knowledge'.

From 100 BC Greece was conquered by the mighty Roman Empire, but even the Romans had respect for the wisdom of the Greeks. This story about a Greek philosopher was first told by Pliny the Younger, a Roman scientist and writer, in the first century. It is one of the oldest recorded ghost stories.

THE HAUNTED HOUSE

The philosopher Athendorus chose his words carefully. He had just arrived in Athens and needed to find a home quickly.

'The house is fine. It's a bit run-down but it's spacious and quiet. However, it's surprisingly cheap. Is there a problem?' Athendorus asked the property agent.

The Parthenon temple in Athens – as it would have looked in the fifth century BC.

HISTORY FACT FILE

Athens reached the height of its power during the fifth century BC. Other city-states paid money to Athens to protect them from attack. With this wealth, the Athenians built beautiful buildings such as the Parthenon temple. Many of these buildings were so admired that their style of architecture is still copied today.

11

This detail from a painting by Raphael shows Plato and Aristotle – two famous philosophers of ancient Athens. Plato's ideas about how to have a fairer society are still studied by political thinkers today.

The agent smiled nervously and said, 'I'm sure it will be perfect. The stories are only rumours. I've never seen anything unusual.'

Athendorus frowned. There *had* to be a catch. 'What are these rumours?' he asked.

'Well,' replied the agent, very reluctantly, 'I've heard that the house is haunted. The ghost is said to be a hideous old man. He has a long beard matted with dirt and his hair is ragged and uncombed. He looks starved and his thin legs are weighed down with heavy shackles and chains. He stumbles and lurches, shaking his fist in the air as if he's angry. When I first tried to let the house, a group of young men hired it for the night as a dare. They laughed at the idea of a ghost. But the next day they were found scared out of their minds. After that, they never had any good luck. Within a year they were all dead, or dying.'

Athendorus listened intently. This was an opportunity not to be missed. The rent was low and if he was brave enough to face the terrors of the supernatural, he could get a bargain.

'I might put up with a quiet ghost, but a noisy, clanking phantom? Now if the price was lower, say half?' Athendorus suggested.

The agent sighed. These philosophers were all the same – full of ideas, but no money. However, the house was a real problem to let. He turned to Athendorus and said, 'Perhaps we can come to an arrangement, sir.'

HISTORY FACT FILE

The Ancient Greeks worshipped many gods and believed in evil spirits. But the philosophers of Athens and other city-states tried to find rational explanations for natural events, rather than relying on superstitious or religious ideas. Aristotle (384–322 BC), tutor to Alexander the Great, was one of the first philosophers to encourage the scientific method of thinking. His rule was: 'Look carefully first, then make your theory'.

AN UNQUIET SPIRIT

Two days later, Athendorus moved into the house. He often worked through the night and he was not going to change his habits now. In fact, he decided to work on a particularly difficult problem. This would stop him imagining things that were not there. And if the worst happened, he would face it. Reason would overcome fear.

Athendorus was absorbed in his calculations when the noise began. Clanking and wailing echoed through the house, getting ever closer. But Athendorus worked on, ignoring the noisy presence. When the ghost came to the study, it saw the philosopher hunched in the lamplight and sensed a new victim. This human would pay for the crime done so long ago.

The spectre shook its chains and moaned fiercely. It waited for the man to flee in terror. But Athendorus paused only to dip his pen in the inkwell. The ghost stopped. What was this? Was the living one deaf? The phantom moved nearer to Athendorus, jabbering wildly and thrashing its chains and shackles.

'Shush!' snapped the philosopher. Inside, Athendorus was quaking and his instincts screamed at him to flee but he would not give in.

The ghost stepped back in surprise. No one had talked to it like this before. In fact, no one had *ever* talked to it. The others had all run away or fainted. Could this be the one it had waited for? The one who would help? The ghost moaned, but a little quieter.

Athendorus wrote furiously for a few minutes and then looked up. 'Well, what do you want?' he demanded, hoping the sweat on his brow didn't show in the lamplight.

This time the phantom beckoned to the philosopher with its bony finger. Athendorus followed it into the garden. The spectre stopped by the shrubbery and gave him a pitiful look. It pointed to the ground and then disappeared. With a sigh of relief, Athendorus marked the spot. That was enough for tonight. Tomorrow he would deal with whatever lay hidden there.

THE DISCOVERY

The next morning the philosopher went to the city magistrates and asked for the garden to be investigated. Below the shrubbery a team of diggers found a skeleton. Rusted chains still held the bones of a prisoner. Was the poor ghost a murder victim or a slave killed by a cruel master? No one could say but at least the remains could now be given a proper burial.

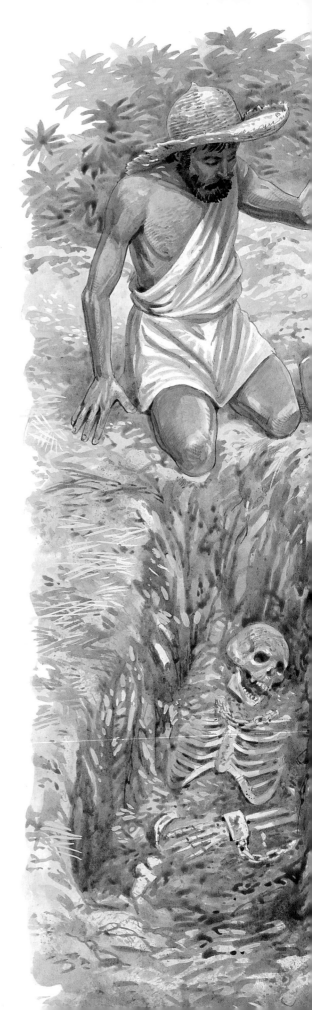

After the skeleton had been laid to rest, the ghost was never seen again. But just to be sure, Athendorus sent for a priest to cleanse the house of unquiet spirits. The philosopher's courage had rescued a troubled ghost but Athendorus did not want any more terrifying encounters with the supernatural.

The bones in Athendorus' garden could well have been those of a murdered slave. Slaves in Ancient Athens had no legal rights. Old slaves might be left to die in the streets and owners could even murder their slaves. Other free men might have disapproved or thought that this was a waste of money, but at the time it was not a crime.

On this piece of Ancient Greek pottery, a girl slave is pouring a drink for her master.

At least half the people in ancient Athens were slaves. Most were captured in war or born to parents who were already slaves. Many slaves were employed in the houses of the rich and were generally well treated. Others were less fortunate. About 20,000 slaves laboured in the silver mines at Laurium. Conditions were dreadful and thousands died of exhaustion while hacking out the silver that made Athens rich.

THE TRAGEDY OF CATHERINE HOWARD

◆ **Henry VIII** is one of England's most famous kings. He was born in 1491 and became king in 1509. His father, Henry Tudor, who became Henry VII, took the throne after defeating Richard III at the Battle of Bosworth in 1485. When Henry VIII became king, he was desperate for a son to succeed him and carry on the Tudor line.

The ruthless Henry VIII ruled England for 38 years.

A SPLENDID PALACE

Hampton Court was built between 1514 and 1520 as the luxurious country house of Cardinal Thomas Wolsey. Wolsey was an important church leader and Chancellor of the Exchequer to King Henry VIII. His new home was built beside the River Thames, a few miles up-river from London, and cost a great deal of money.

The house was designed to show off Wolsey's wealth and influence but Henry became resentful and jealous of his upstart chancellor. Anxious to please the king, Wolsey reluctantly handed his beautiful home over to him. This grand gesture did not please Henry for long. Wolsey was arrested for treason and died on the way to London to stand trial. Henry happily took over the house. He made it even more luxurious and lived in it for much of his reign.

TO HAVE A SON

Henry VIII had six wives. He divorced his first wife after falling in love with Anne Boleyn. When Anne first came to Hampton Court Palace, Henry loved her so much that he had their intertwined initials 'H' and 'A' carved on the walls.

But Henry desperately wanted a son, and when Anne gave birth to a daughter, Elizabeth, he had her sent to trial and found guilty of adultery. She was beheaded and Henry was now free to marry again. He married Jane Seymour, and at last, to his great joy, she gave him his long-awaited son, Edward, in 1537. Sadly Jane died soon after childbirth.

Henry married three more times. He was disappointed with his fourth wife so he divorced her. His fifth wife was Catherine Howard, whose sad story is told below. Henry's last wife, Catherine Parr, outlived him.

CATHERINE'S DOOMED MARRIAGE

Catherine Howard first caught Henry's eye in 1539, when she was appointed maid of honour to his fourth wife, the German princess Anne of Cleves. The king's marriage to Anne was a failure from the beginning. When Anne arrived in England, Henry was shocked to find her plain and dull.

In contrast, Catherine was pretty and high-spirited. She was only nineteen and Henry was dazzled by her. By then he was forty-nine, overweight and often ill, but in her company he seemed to regain his energy.

In 1509 Henry married his first wife, the Spanish princess Catherine of Aragon. Only one of Catherine's children survived, a daughter called Mary. Henry then fell in love with Anne Boleyn. He wanted to divorce Catherine and marry Anne. The Catholic Church would not allow Henry to divorce his wife, so he set up the Church of England and made himself head of it. Then he ordered his bishops and Parliament to pass the Divorce Act. This event triggered the Protestant Reformation in England. This was a time of bitter rivalry between Catholics and Protestants in some parts of Europe.

Catherine's relatives took advantage of the situation and at every opportunity they dangled the young girl before the eager king. They even arranged secret meetings between the lovers.

In July 1540 Henry divorced Anne of Cleves and married Catherine. For a few months Henry was like a man reborn, rising at 5 am and hunting until mid-morning. At night he danced and banqueted with his new bride. Catherine loved the attention of her doting husband, and his presents of beautiful jewellery.

However, as time passed the queen became bored with her old, ugly and moody husband. She looked for excitement, and a year after her marriage she fell in love with a handsome courtier, Thomas Culpeper. She had a passionate love affair with him. She also offered a place at court to her former lover, Francis Dereham.

Catherine should have known that it was impossible to keep things secret in the gossipy world of the palace. Henry was furious when he was told about his queen's misdeeds. He had been betrayed, and now he would have his revenge.

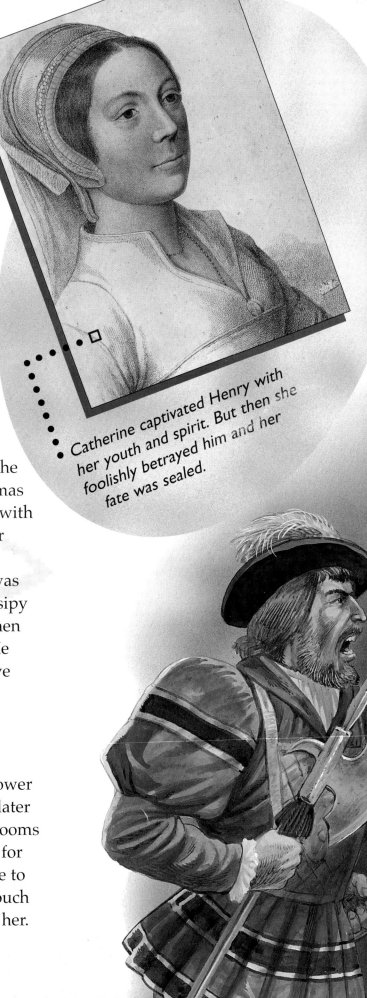

Catherine captivated Henry with her youth and spirit. But then she foolishly betrayed him and her fate was sealed.

A PLEA FOR MERCY

Culpeper and Dereham were sent to the Tower of London, where they were tortured and later beheaded. Catherine was confined to her rooms on a charge of treason. This was too much for her to bear. She was terrified and desperate to see Henry. She felt that if only she could touch him and plead with him he would forgive her.

Catherine knew that Henry went to mass every day in the Royal Chapel at one end of the Long Gallery. This was only a short dash from her rooms at the other end of the gallery. So she summoned up her strength and broke away from the guards, running for her life to the chapel door. She hammered on the door, sobbing and begging for mercy.

Inside the chapel the king heard her anguished cries but coldly continued his prayers. He had no mercy to show her. The guards dragged her away, struggling and screaming. Catherine Howard was beheaded on 12 February 1542.

A painting from 1816 showing the Royal Chapel at Hampton Court Palace.

Catherine Howard's story is well known, so perhaps sightings of her ghost are just in the imagination of visitors. However, some ghost-hunters believe that tragic human events are recorded by buildings. Under certain conditions that are not yet understood, events can be played back. It may be that Catherine's last dash to see Henry has been rerunning for over 450 years.

THE GHOST OF THE LONG GALLERY

It is said that the ghosts of Anne Boleyn (in a blue dress) and Jane Seymour (holding a lighted candle) have been seen in the corridors of Hampton Court Palace. But it is in the Long Gallery that the most terrifying haunting has been witnessed.

The incident only lasts for a few seconds but it is said to chill the blood of observers. A young woman runs down the gallery as if her life is in danger, her long hair streaming out behind her. The woman's frantic dash ends at the Royal chapel.

Some people have sensed a coldness outside the chapel door and heard tormented cries. Is this the forlorn ghost of Catherine Howard begging for mercy?

THE PHANTOM SOLDIERS OF EDGEHILL

THE ENGLISH CIVIL WAR

In 1642 a civil war broke out in England. At that time England was ruled by King Charles I. The country was divided between those who supported the king, called royalists, and those who believed the king was too powerful and wanted Parliament to have more say in governing the people.

On 23 October 1642 the two sides faced each other across gently sloping ground at Edgehill, on the borders of Warwickshire and Northamptonshire. The royalist army (or Cavaliers) occupied the higher ground, looking down the slope towards the parliamentary army (the Roundheads).

Men gripped their weapons tightly: swords that could sever limbs; pikes that could gash deep into bodies; muskets with ammunition that could break bones and leave terrible wounds. Behind the lines the surgeon waited, ready to saw off broken limbs while the screaming patient was held down.

A matchlock musket from the seventeenth century. Muskets were long and heavy. They were difficult to load, aim and fire.

This picture shows the matchlock's firing mechanism. The serpent on the right is a vice that holds a burning match in its jaws. The vice was often made to look like a monster's head.

HISTORY FACT FILE

The English Civil War (1642–45) broke out between King Charles I and Parliament. Charles believed that only the king had the right to rule and Parliament was there merely to advise him. But Parliament had grown in power and it demanded that the king should rule through its members (MPs). The problem came to a head when Charles found himself short of money to fight a war against Scotland. Only Parliament could help raise huge amounts of money but it would not agree to do so unless the king gave up some of his powers. When Charles refused both sides prepared for war.

21

THE REAL BATTLE

A trumpet sounded from the royalist ranks. The king's cavalry, led by the brave and headstrong Prince Rupert, began to trot and then to gallop towards the parliamentary lines. Nothing could stop the rush of Rupert's troops. The flanks of the parliamentary army were scattered but the centre held firm.

A desperate struggle now took place as the parliamentary forces at the centre stood fast against the royalist foot soldiers. The king's standard was lost and his commander lay dying. When Rupert realized the plight of the royalist foot soldiers, he bravely led his cavalry in an attack on the parliamentary troops. The standard was retaken, complete with the severed hand of its standard-bearer, Sir Edmund Verney, still grasping the shaft. As darkness fell the two armies drew apart.

At first the war went well for the king as he had trained soldiers and the most able generals on his side. The battle at Edgehill was one of the first battles of the Civil War. The parliamentary leaders, including Oliver Cromwell, learnt many lessons from this battle. Cromwell trained a cavalry unit that earned a reputation for discipline and toughness in battle – the 'Ironsides'.

Van Dyck's famous portrait of King Charles I (1600–49).

Backed by the wealth of London and commanding a well-trained army, the parliamentary forces eventually won the war and captured the king. Charles I was beheaded on 30 January 1649.

Slowly the field returned to its former use. Cattle and sheep grazed on it. Birds sang and swooped over the waving grass. Insects buzzed and darted here and there. But the earth was merely sleeping.

A GHOSTLY BATTLE

Just over a year after the Battle of Edgehill, on Christmas Eve 1643, some shepherds were on their way home. Their route took them past the scene of the battle. As the shepherds came over the rise they looked down the slope into the valley below. They were amazed to see, lit by the silvery moonlight, two armies locked in battle. They saw men's agonized faces, with mouths open in silent screams as swords and pikes tore flesh and shattered bones. Flags rippled in an imaginary breeze, for the air was as still as death.

Above the scene of carnage a huge standard fluttered over the great battlefield, and clutching its shaft was a hand, severed at the wrist and dripping blood. News of the phantom soldiers spread and others came to witness the ghostly battle.

THE SEARCH FOR THE SEVERED HAND

It is believed that the ghost of the standard-bearer, Sir Edmund Verney, still bears witness to the events of that terrible battle. When the parliamentary troops captured Sir Edmund, they demanded that he give up the standard. He refused, saying, 'My life is my own, but my standard is the king's.' So he was killed. But the Roundheads could not prise Sir Edmund's hand from the shaft of the standard and had to hack off his hand to free it.

Sir Edmund's body was buried in an unmarked grave but his severed hand was sent to his home, Claydon House, where it was buried in the family vault with his signet ring still in place.

The original Claydon House was pulled down. The present house occupying the site was built in 1768 and there are many stories about its ghost. A carpenter who was working on the demolition of the enormous ballroom chanced to look up and saw a strangely dressed man standing nearby, looking sadly at the ruins. When the carpenter called to the stranger, the figure disappeared.

HISTORY FACT FILE

Oliver Cromwell ruled England until his death in 1658. In 1660 the monarchy was restored under Charles II, the eldest son of Charles I.

On the orders of Charles II, Cromwell's mouldering corpse was dug up. The head was chopped off and stuck on a pole on London Bridge, where it stayed for many years.

In 1892 the daughter of Sir Harry Verney also noticed a ghostly figure. She said, 'I ran up the Red Stairs at Claydon House, and turned left and left again on the first landing and then took a few steps towards the Cedar Room. I noticed with surprise that a man was halfway down from the upper floor. I ran to look more closely but he was gone. I saw him on the third step of the second flight, as he was coming down. He was tall and slender and wore a long, black cloak, beneath the hem of which peeped the tip of his sword. He carried a black hat with a white feather gracefully curled around the crown.'

In 1923 a forester's wife heard heavy footsteps in the corridor when the house was supposed to be empty.

Perhaps the ghost of Sir Edmund still searches the house for his lost hand while the phantom battle at Edgehill rages silently on.

COMFORT'S CURSE

A WITCH TRIAL IN NEW ENGLAND

An historic trial took place in the American town of Bucksport, Maine, in New England in 1692.

In the small courtroom, the black-robed magistrate glared at the frail old woman in the dock.

'Comfort Ainsworth, rise to your feet,' he commanded. 'You have been found guilty of witchcraft. This court has heard testimony against you that you did mutter curses upon your neighbours that their very ears should erupt in blood; that a monstrous demon, black-hooded and ten feet tall, was seen at your doorway; that you did fly unnaturally in the heavens and made animals help you in your evil work. In these things the court judges you to be guilty. We are told by Scripture: "suffer not witches to live among you". You shall be taken from this place and kept secure until tomorrow, when you shall be hanged by the neck until you are dead…'

Sitting in the court that day was Colonel Buck. He nodded in approval towards the magistrate, a smile of satisfaction on his face. Time and again he had encouraged his fellow villagers of Bucksport to root out witches, as their neighbours in nearby Salem had done. And what horror had been uncovered in the midst of *that* God-fearing community.

HISTORY FACT FILE

Witch hunts were common in parts of Europe during the seventeenth century. Occasionally they took place in the newly settled colonies on the east coast of North America. In 1692 a terrifying witch hunt broke out in the village of Salem in Massachusetts, New England. Many of the settlers there were Puritan refugees, escaping religious persecution in Europe. Puritans were strict Protestants who believed they had to continually guard against the temptations of the devil. They thought the devil was capable of using people (often women) to do his evil work.

Salem village was the scene of the worst witch trials at that time.

Salem was changing from a group of scattered farms to a busy port, and the older community felt threatened by the changes. These older villagers knew everything about each other's business – family rivalries, scandals and imagined insults were always present. They were also extremely religious and believed they were surrounded by evil. In these circumstances, it was sometimes difficult for them to distinguish between innocence and guilt.

THE CURSE

Colonel Buck had 'discovered the devil' in Bucksport. He had accused ninety-year-old Comfort Ainsworth of being a witch and had brought her in front of the magistrate. Buck had stirred up the villagers to a frenzy. He had told the witnesses what their answers should be, and throughout the trial he had whispered advice to the magistrate. It had taken the jury less than one minute to convict old Comfort.

Standing silent in the dock until this moment, the old woman seemed to uncoil her bent and twisted frame. Her eyes bulged in their sockets and spittle bubbled from the corner of her mouth. She stretched out a bony finger in the direction of Colonel Buck.

'In all my life I have cursed no other being, but today I lay a curse upon you,' Comfort cried. 'Mark this and mark it well. I shall walk upon your grave and leave the footprint of my passing forever upon you.'

The next morning the exhausted woman was lifted into the noose hanging from the gallows and the life was choked from her body.

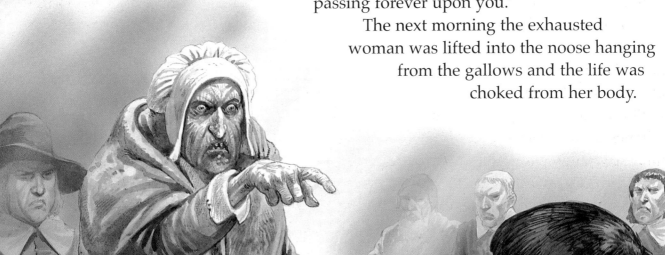

COMFORT'S REVENGE

The fear of Comfort's curse seemed to settle on everyone in the village. Very few people turned out to see the old woman's execution, not even Colonel Buck, who had worked so hard to get her convicted of witchcraft.

A few days later the colonel complained of stomach pains and was unable to eat. He became ill and feverish, and cried out that he could see the wrinkled face of Comfort Ainsworth in front of his eyes. He tried to beat away the phantom with his hands, but again and again it returned and whispered the curse in Buck's ear.

Colonel Buck wasted away until his body seemed no larger than the skinny frame of old Comfort. Just before he died he said to his family, 'She visits me and gives me no rest. I see my days are now few. I must rest in peace. My grave must be covered in flawless marble that is incapable of being stained.'

THE GHOSTLY FOOTPRINT

The next day Colonel Buck died. His relatives promptly told the stonemason to provide a slab of the best marble for his grave.

Frenzy at a witch trial. The girl on the floor is 'possessed by the devil' and is pointing to other 'guilty' people.

28

As the stonemason chipped the colonel's name into the marble slab, a stooped shadow crossed it. The stone began to discolour, leaving a brown stain in the form of a footprint. No amount of rubbing with a whetstone could remove the mark. The stonemason fled, terrified, and told Buck's relatives what he had seen. They made him promise to tell no one, and ordered him to bury the marble slab and cut a new stone.

The new marble stone was put into position and the relatives sighed with relief. But a few days later, frightened villagers begged Buck's relatives to come to the cemetery to see what had happened. As the relatives neared the grave and the stone came into view, they saw at once that their plan had failed. There, imprisoned and accusing in the stone, was the mark of Comfort's bony footprint.

You may visit the graveyard, and in the softly stirring breeze that breaks the silence of the dead you may hear the whispered curse of Comfort, as she walks upon the colonel's grave.

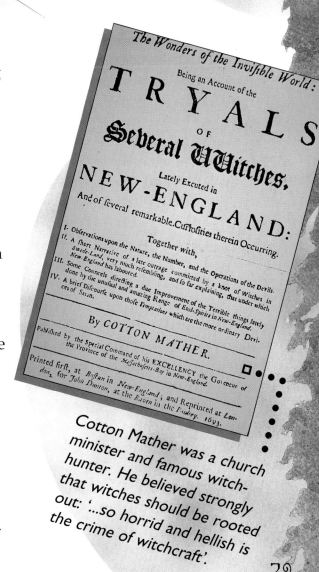

The Wonders of the Invisible World:

Being an Account of the

TRYALS

OF

Several Witches,

Lately Executed in

NEW-ENGLAND:

And of several remarkable.Curiosities therein Occurring.

Together with,

I. Observations upon the Nature, the Number, and the Operations of the Devils.
II. A short Narrative of a late outrage committed by a knot of Witches in Swede-Land, very much resembling, and so far explaining, that under which New-England has laboured.
III. Some Councels directing a due Improvement of the Terrible things lately done by the unusual and amazing Range of Evil-Spirits in New-England.
IV. A brief Discourse upon those Temptations which are the more ordinary Devices of Satan.

By COTTON MATHER.

Published by the Special Command of his EXCELLENCY the Governour of the Province of the Massachusetts-Bay in New-England.

Printed first, at Boston in New-England; and Reprinted at London, for John Dunton, at the Raven in the Poultry. 1693.

Cotton Mather was a church minister and famous witch-hunter. He believed strongly that witches should be rooted out: '...so horrid and hellish is the crime of witchcraft'.

GLOSSARY

☐ **Adultery** Having a love affair with someone when married to someone else.

☐ **Besieging** Surrounding a town with troops so that nothing and no one can get in or out.

☐ **Biology** The study of plants and animals.

☐ **Cardinal** A high-ranking official in the Catholic Church.

☐ **Carnage** Terrible slaughter in battle.

☐ **Cavalry** Troops mounted on horseback.

☐ **Chancellor of the Exchequer** The minister in charge of the finances of the UK.

☐ **Civil war** A war between two groups within one country.

☐ **Dock** The enclosure in a criminal court where the accused person stands.

☐ **Flanks** The right and left sides of an army.

☐ **Heresy** An opinion that is against the commonly held beliefs of the time.

☐ **Martyr** A person who suffers or is put to death for their beliefs.

☐ **Muskets** Heavy, long-barrelled guns used by foot soldiers.

☐ **Persecution** Ill-treatment of people, especially because of their religion or race.

☐ **Phantom** A ghost or spirit.

☐ **Prejudice** Unfair or unreasonable opinion.

☐ **Psychic** Relating to powers outside the range of normal experience.

☐ **Puritans** Protestants who wished to 'purify' the Church of England, removing any trace of the Catholic religion.

☐ **Rational** Based on common sense.

☐ **Reformation** The introduction of the Protestant religion in certain European countries.

☐ **Shrine** A place of worship.

☐ **Spectre** A ghost or spirit.

☐ **Standard** The monarch's special flag.

☐ **Supernatural** Relating to something that cannot be explained by natural laws.

☐ **Testimony** Evidence, usually given in court.

☐ **Treason** Disloyalty to a ruler.

☐ **Whetstone** A fine-grained stone usually used by crafts people to sharpen their tools.

FURTHER READING

The Encyclopedia of Ghosts and Spirits by John and Anne Spencer (Headline, 1992)
Mysterious World: The Supernatural by Ivor Baddiel and Tracey Blezard (Macdonald Young Books, 1998)
The Paranormal: An Illustrated Encyclopedia by Stuart Gordon (Headline, 1992)
The Unexplained: Hauntings by Peter Hepplewhite and Neil Tonge (Hamlyn, 1997)

● ●□ Agincourt, Battle of 7
Ainscough, Alan 10
Ainsworth, Comfort 26–29
America 26, 28
Arc, Joan of 6, 8–10
architecture, Ancient Greek 11
Athendorus 11–15
Athens 11, 12, 15

● ●□ Buck, Colonel 26, 27, 28
Bucksport, Maine (New England) 26, 27, 28
Burgundy, Duke of 7, 9

● ●□ Charles, King
        Charles I 21, 23
        Charles II 24
        Charles VI 7
        Charles VII 7, 8
Church, the 10, 17
Claydon House 24, 25
Cromwell, Oliver 22, 24
Culpeper, Thomas 18
curse (Comfort Ainsworth) 27, 28, 29

● ●□ Dereham, Francis 18

● ●□ Edgehill, Battle of 21–22, 23, 25
England 7, 9, 16, 17, 24
English Civil War 21
execution (Joan of Arc) 10

● ●□ France 6, 7, 8, 9, 10

● ●□ Germany 10
ghosts 12–15, 20, 23, 24, 25, 28
Greece, Ancient 11, 12

● ●□ Hampton Court Palace 16, 19, 20
haunted house (Athens) 11–15

Henry, King
    Henry V 7
    Henry VII 16
    Henry VIII 16–20
        wives of:
            Aragon, Catherine of 17
            Boleyn, Anne 16, 17, 20
            Cleves, Anne of 17, 18
            Howard, Catherine 17–20
            Parr, Catherine 17
            Seymour, Jane 17, 20
Hundred Years' War 7, 9

● ●□ mines, silver (Ancient Athens) 15
muskets 21

● ●□ Orleans, Battle of 8–9

● ●□ Parliament (English Civil War) 21
parliamentary army (Roundheads) 21–24
Parthenon 11
philosophers, Ancient Greek 11, 12
Puritans 26

● ●□ religion 8, 10, 17, 26, 27
royalists (Cavaliers) 21, 22
Rupert, Prince 22

● ●□ Salem, Massachusetts (New England) 26, 27, 28
slaves 15

● ●□ trials 6, 9–10, 26, 27, 28

● ●□ Verney, Sir Edmund 22, 24, 25

● ●□ witch hunts 26, 28, 29
witch trials 26, 27, 28
Wolsey, Cardinal Thomas 16

GH10

(

First published in 1999 by Macdonald Young Books,
an imprint of Wayland Publishers Limited

Text and illustrations
© Macdonald Young Books 1999

Macdonald Young Books
61 Western Road, Hove,
East Sussex, BN3 1JD

Look for Macdonald Young Books
on the internet at:
http://www.myb.co.uk

Series editor: Rosie Nixon
Editor: Annie Scothern
Designer: Dalia Hartman
Illustrator: Peter Dennis
Consultant: Peter Hicks

Picture acknowledgements: Bibliotheque Nationale Paris/e.t.
archives 7, e.t. archives 19, Louvre/e.t. archives 15, James
Davis Travel Photography 16, Peter Newark's American
Pictures 26, 28, 29, Hulton Getty 10, 11, 18, Royal
Armouries 21, Hever Castle Ltd, Kent/Bridgeman Art
Library, London/New York 16, Vatican Museums and
Galleries. Vatican City/Bridgeman Art Library/New York
12, Bibliotheque Nationale, Paris/Bridgeman Art Library,
London/New York 8, Philip Mould, Historical Portraits Ltd,
London/Bridgeman Art Library, London/New York 23,
Wayland Picture Library 24.

British Library Cataloguing in Publication Data
Hepplewhite, Peter
    Ghostly Tales from Long Ago. - (Haunted History)
    1. Ghosts - Juvenile literature 2. Haunted places -
    Juvenile literature
    I.Title II.Tonge, Neil
    133.1'09

ISBN 07500 2642 1

Printed and bound in Portugal by Edições ASA